Six Ways To Enjoy This Strategic Coach Book

Text 60 Minutes	The length of [illegible]ed on the time in the air of a flight [illegible]oronto and Chicago. Start reading as you take off and finish the book by the time you land. Just the right length for the 21st-century reader.
Cartoons 30 Minutes	You can also gain a complete overview of the ideas in this book by looking at the cartoons and reading the captions. We find the cartoons have made our Strategic Coach concepts accessible to readers as young as eight years old.
Audio 120 Minutes	The audio recording that accompanies this book is not just a recitation of the printed words but an in-depth commentary that expands each chapter's mindset into new dimensions. Download the audio at **strategiccoach.com/go/nbb**
Video 30 Minutes	Our video interviews about the concepts in the book deepen your understanding of the mindsets. If you combine text, cartoons, audio, and video, your understanding of the ideas will be 10x greater than you would gain from reading only. Watch the videos at **strategiccoach.com/go/nbb**
Scorecard 10 Minutes	Score your Not Being Bothered Mindset at **strategiccoach.com/go/nbb**. First, score yourself on where you are now, and then fill in where you want to be a year from now.
ebook 1 Minute	After absorbing the fundamental ideas of the Not Being Bothered concept, you can quickly and easily share them by sending the ebook version to as many other individuals as you desire. Direct them to **strategiccoach.com/go/nbb**

Thanks to the Creative Team:

Adam Morrison
Kerri Morrison
Hamish MacDonald
Shannon Waller
Jennifer Bhatthal
Suvi Siu
Christine Nishino
Willard Bond
Peggy Lam
Alex Varley

Not Being Bothered

It happens to the best of us. You find yourself reacting emotionally to a situation or problem, and suddenly, you're stuck. You don't know how to move forward. You feel paralyzed and unable to think clearly, make decisions, or take action.

You're bothered.

Find out why certain problems bother you while others don't, what causes you to feel stuck, and the one question to ask yourself to immediately get unstuck and moving forward.

Cartoons by Hamish MacDonald.

Printed in Toronto, Canada. The Strategic Coach Inc., 33 Fraser Avenue, Suite 201, Toronto, Ontario, M6K 3J9.

If you would like further information about The Strategic Coach® Program or other Strategic Coach® services and products, please telephone 416.531.7399 or 1.800.387.3206.

Library and Archives Canada Cataloguing in Publication

Title: Not being bothered : increasing your achievement during distracting times / Dan Sullivan ;
cartoons by Hamish MacDonald.
Names: Sullivan, Dan, 1944- author.
Identifiers: Canadiana 20220225451 | ISBN 9781897239803 (softcover)
Subjects: LCSH: Distraction (Psychology) | LCSH: Attention. | LCSH: Achievement motivation. | LCSH:
Success in business.
Classification: LCC BF323.D5 S85 2022 | DDC 153.7/33—dc23

Contents

Introduction 6
Success In A "Bothered World"

Chapter 1 12
Anything Can Be A Bother

Chapter 2 18
90% Of Any Problem

Chapter 3 24
Everybody Has Bothers

Chapter 4 30
If You Weren't Bothered

Chapter 5 36
90% Of Any Solution

Chapter 6 42
Bothered People Congregate

Chapter 7 48
Transforming Your Bothers

Chapter 8 54
Loving Your Bothers

Conclusion 60
Freedom In A Bothered World

The Strategic Coach Program 66
For Ambitious, Collaborative Entrepreneurs

Introduction

Success In A "Bothered World"

You realize that a growing population multiplied by communication platforms generates a "bothered world" that you can turn to your advantage.

Most successful people's daily lives are filled with the latest news about how other people are "being bothered" in old and new ways.

As more and more people are connecting through new kinds of communication technologies, especially social media, there is even more to be bothered by. And social media's creators are competing to capture and sell the attention of as many people as possible.

When you're bothered—that is, annoyed, irritated, or upset—you lose your ability to think clearly, make decisions, and take action. You're in a confused state, and it usually comes on by surprise. And though people have the tendency to attribute this feeling to some external cause, it's always something that takes place on the inside.

While the world around you is becoming more and more "bothered," it's time to turn that "bother" to your advantage by dealing with it in a way that always leads to successful learning, decision making, action, and achievements.

Increasingly complicated reality.

You realize that the world is continually changing in ways you don't fully understand, and what you do understand tells you, realistically, that you can't change how the world is changing—except when it comes to yourself. You can continually improve how you respond to living in a bothered world.

Anything can be a bother. A bother is an emotional reaction to a problem or difficult situation. So the way to deal with it is, when you experience a bother, compare it to another situation where you were bothered in the past. You'll find that it wasn't the *experience* that bothered you, but something closer to home.

Proof of this is that there are things that used to bother you and now don't. This shows a separation between your outside experience and your inside experience. It's not the outside situation that's responsible for the bother, because then the outside situation would always cause the same amount of bother inside you. Rather, it's the way you *respond* to situations that leaves you bothered—or not.

"Being bothered" is the news.

What used to be called the daily, up-to-date news is increasingly not about the world itself, but about all the ways that large numbers of people are bothered by changes in the world. Your first mindset improvement, therefore, is to ignore all the "bothered news."

More and more, the purpose of the news is not to inform you by simply presenting the facts, but to shock you. The news media wants to trigger you into feeling a negative emotional reaction, as the more people they trigger, the more viewers they get.

The people who are communicating in a way that bothers a large number of people are very bothered people themselves. If you're not bothered, you won't try to bother other people.

Connectivity addiction.

Many of the daily things that bother you are the result of inviting the bothers into your life. Your use of communication technology is one way of doing this. To the degree that you think it's crucial to be connected with the world, you will be bothered.

Many people can't stand being separated from their social media apps. They want to be engaging all the time because they've become dependent on an outside source to trigger certain kinds of emotions. They get excited, they get angry, but they are only reacting. They're not managing their own emotions.

When you have a bothersome experience, there is a rush of adrenaline, making you excited. For most people, it's only that stimulation from the outside that actually gets their adrenaline going. But it's important to train yourself to use your own internal ability to manage your emotions. You have to learn how to trigger those emotions for yourself without relying on something external.

Changing your mindset.

It's easier and faster to change your mindset than to change the bothersome behavior of other people. This process of successful improvement will continually happen in the time that it takes to read this book, listen to the accompanying audio, or watch the videos. In a couple of hours, you'll be less bothered.

Your mindset is already starting to shift at this point, and with every chapter, you'll experience an additional shift.

Being bothered means you're lacking the capability to *not* be bothered. It means you're dependent on others. Your sense of security and progress is tied to everyone else's sense of security and progress. So when things don't go as planned, you don't have an independent sense of being able to create your own security, direction, and capability. But once you have the capability to not be bothered, you can create a sense of personal security, direction, and progress for yourself.

Every bother is an opportunity.

The mindset transformation you'll experience is not just about eliminating bothers as a problem but actually turning more and more of your bothers into practical opportunities. Very quickly, you'll view any bother you encounter as a resource.

The world will never run out of bother, and so being able to transform bother into a practical opportunity with no cost to you at all is an invaluable skill.

While you continually perform this transformation, the majority of other people aren't going to notice or pay attention to it because they're too caught up in being bothered. Your new capability will therefore be a free, invisible resource.

In the following chapters, I'll show you how recognizing that you're feeling bothered and understanding that it's coming from the inside, not the outside, is half the battle. Then, I'll share one simple question to ask yourself whenever you're bothered that will jolt you out of the bother so you can move forward with creative action.

GROWING SUCCESS...
BOTHER
BOTHER
BOTHER
BOTHER
BOTHER
BOTHER
BOTHER

...IN A WORLD OF BOTHER
BOTHER

Chapter 1

Anything Can Be A Bother

You're surprised to discover that you've always been bothered by many different things, almost too many to count.

It's important to recognize the countless bothers you've experienced in your life and that anything can be a bother, because you can now begin to understand where your bothers come from.

For example, you realize that a particular situation that is suddenly bothering you today never bothered you in the past. And something that bothered you last week isn't bothering you today. The same thing is true about particular people. Some may have bothered you in the past, but they don't bother you today.

So, taking all of these experiences into account over your entire lifetime, it begins to look like almost anything can bother you. Now that you've discovered this, you won't forget it. And because you won't forget it, it will transform how you handle all your bothers in the future.

Never learn.

Some people never come to grips with their bothers. They never learn from the experiences that annoy, irritate, and upset them. Just waking up in the morning reminds them of everything that bothers them. They try to cope with many different kinds of distractions and activities to help them forget about all their bothers, but none of them work for very long. Soon enough, everything they hope will free them from their bothers only turns into the next thing that bothers them.

What causes them?

But you now realize that your bothers don't actually come from anywhere outside of you. When you compare any experience that bothers you today with the same or similar experience that happened in the past, you see that the experiences themselves cannot explain why you're bothered.

In fact, you'll find that the only factor that's present in every single situation is you. What this means is that the answer as to why you're bothered by different people or situations at different times can be found inside yourself, not by simply looking at the outside circumstances that are present when you're bothered.

You're in your own universe inside of the big universe, and you can be in control of your own universe.

Today, not yesterday.

You've been puzzled when you've thought about how things that didn't bother you before suddenly do. Someone who never bothered you before suddenly does. And the reverse is also true—you're fascinated by the fact that situations and people that bothered you in the past no longer do.

When you first encounter a bother, 90 percent of the problem is that you get caught up in the emotions of it. What you need to do is ask yourself, *"If this didn't bother me, how would I handle it?"* Your emotions can't answer that question. Your emotions are alerts and censors, but they're not problem solvers that can create a course of action to solve something.

Only your intellect can do that. So, what you do by asking this question is break the spell and give control back to your brain. Your brain will provide suggestions as to what you can do, and if you go ahead and take those actions and achieve something, you'll likely discover that you're no longer bothered by what was bothering you before.

And even more than that, you most likely won't be bothered again if you find yourself in a similar situation in the future. That's what you gain when you achieve some usefulness out of being bothered.

All the same.

Your whole lifetime's collection of bothers, for as long as you can remember, seem to be remarkably the same. That is, almost anything that happens to you can bother you. And almost anything that's bothered you can stop bothering you.

You're starting to see that throughout your entire life, every bother you've experienced was strictly your doing. No one else had a hand in it. And you can see that the same is also true for everybody else, with them being responsible for every one of their own bothers throughout their entire lives.

Some people react to their experiences of being bothered by being loud about it, which can give the impression that their bother is a more serious situation than it is. But you have no need or desire to shout about it when you experience bother.

Changing your meaning.

In a very important and permanent way, you're fundamentally changing the meaning of your whole life up until now.

And what you're changing in your thinking about your past, you realize, automatically applies to your future. With one shift of mindset, you're changing who you think you are.

For a lot of people, the main thing in their life is everything that's ever bothered them since they became conscious. And a lot of people react to feeling bothered by trying to eliminate all the factors outside of themselves that make them feel bothered.

You, on the other hand, now know that all of the bother you experience comes not from the outside, but from inside yourself, and instead of wasting your powerful emotions by focusing on outside factors, you're going to use them to produce progress in your life.

Liberating your future.

You now know, even this early in this book, that if *anything* can be a bother to you, then the same thing is true for everyone else. What this means is that other people are not the cause of your bothers, and you've never been—and never will be—the cause of anyone else's bothers. This is enormously liberating!

You can now feel the freedom of knowing that you *are*, you *have been*, and you *will be* responsible only for your own bothers, not for anyone else's. And it's equally liberating to know that no one else has caused or will cause any of your bothers. You are in control, and you can choose right now to make progress every quarter in the way you deal with being bothered.

THE BOTHERS...
TRAVEL
WAITING
SHOULD
EVENTS
PEOPLE
PLACES
DISAPPOINTMENTS
GOSSIP
MEMORIES

...ARE ENDLESS
RUDENESS
WEATHER
COMMUNICATION
WORRIES
NEWS
SURPRISES
FAILURES
ITCHES
BOREDOM

Chapter 2

90% Of Any Problem

You're excited to realize that almost every problem you face is only a problem because you're letting it bother you.

The daily news is filled with stories about how other people are "being bothered" in old and new ways. The global communications universe is filled up 24/7 with lots of information, and much of it is about the amazing number of problems that are bothering an amazing number of people.

You used to be caught up in this bother yourself. But then you realized a simple secret that's vastly reducing the number of things that bother you. And it's also reducing the number of things you think of as problems. Your secret, which is now becoming an amazing daily skill, is that you can use every bother in every area of your life as raw material for successful breakthroughs.

Being responsive.

Instead of putting up with things that bother you as so many people do, you have a proactive approach to dealing with bothers. And your confidence will be greater every time you find yourself in a situation facing a similar bother. Instead of being reactive, which means you're not in control of the circumstances, you're responsive, which means you're bringing your entire set of existing capabilities to the situation. And then from responsiveness, you become transformative and develop brand *new* capabilities.

By changing the way you look at things, you can turn a negative into a positive. When you change your thinking and your attitude, your emotional state changes. As bothers are usually emotional, by owning your response to them, you take responsibility for them. You accept that a negative element is present, but you don't have to be negative in the way you deal with it. You can choose to be creative.

Being bothered is a problem.

You realize that the world is continually changing in ways you don't fully understand. And what you do understand is changing in ways you didn't expect. It's the experience of things changing—in confusing and unexpected ways—that bothers you. Change isn't the problem. Being bothered is.

It all comes down to how you deal with outside experiences. Even if the outside world were somehow rearranged to be just what you wanted, you would still struggle if you didn't have a handle on dealing with your own experience.

Now that you recognize this, you can always turn outside experiences into new skills and capabilities. You learn by transforming the bother, not by avoiding the bother.

Unlike bureaucratic institutions that aim to control their environment, as entrepreneurs, we're capable of handling change, creating change, normalizing change, and adapting to change.

Inside, not outside.

You remember changes happening in your life that didn't bother you. You took in the situation and responded in successful, even enjoyable, ways. This tells you that the problem isn't what's happening outside of you. It's what happens inside of you whenever you don't respond successfully to outside change.

When something unexpected happens, you won't waste time wishing things would go back to normal. You have an approach that always leads to growth, so every stage for you is normal: you consider it normal when things are going along as is, you consider it normal when you're successfully dealing with unexpected circumstances, and you consider it normal when you've jumped to a new level of capability afterward.

Stuck and frustrated.

You can now see that every time you feel like you're not successful in responding to changing circumstances, you're bothered. You're bothered because you feel stuck. You're bothered because you feel less capable. You're bothered because you're frustrated and can't see a way forward.

What's more, when you're stuck, you feel like you've actually lost ground. You had a vision of the ideal, and it turned out not to be true. And when you're stuck in the bother, it prevents you from responding creatively.

But you can look forward to never feeling stuck again. The kinds of circumstances and situations that used to leave you feeling stuck and frustrated will now excite you because you'll see new opportunities to make progress. Things that used to bother you are now opportunities to transform.

You're always the cause.

There's a secret here that explains everything that bothers you and what's happening every time you're bothered. Your feeling bothered is always caused by your not feeling successful. It isn't any outside change that's causing the problem that bothers you. You're the cause of all your bothers.

When you're thinking that there's nothing you can decide, nothing you can communicate, and no action you can take, you feel a lack of success. You feel stuck. The way to get out of it is to accept that you're the one doing it, and decide to stop doing it to yourself.

Remind yourself of what your goal is in the situation, and if you know that one method won't work, then figure out what to try next. Being bothered prevents you from taking action, but taking action breaks the bother.

Your bother, your solution.

You're suddenly struck by a possibility: if you were to decide, just for an experiment, to take responsibility for everything that bothers you, just for today, perhaps some of your outside problems would diminish—maybe even disappear. It's a fascinating possible solution and certainly worth a try.

What makes you a unique individual is your relationship to your bothers. If you give in to your bothers and allow them to keep you from moving forward and succeeding, then that's who you are. If you always transform your bothers into some new form of action, then that's who you are.

And every day, including today, the kind of relationship you have with your bothers is always entirely your choice. The choice you have to make is between giving up and feeling stuck and frustrated—and taking action and feeling successful.

YOUR BOTHERS...
BOTHER
BOTHER
BOTHER
BOTHER
BOTHER

...ARE THE PROBLEM

Chapter 3

Everybody Has Bothers

You increasingly understand that everyone you know has things that bother them — and that their bothers are different from yours.

Everyone has bothers, and that includes you. We're all the same in that respect. But where we're not the same, where everybody is different, is that each of us has uniquely different things that bother us.

Therefore, each of us is on our own in relation to our bothers. You understand this, you accept it, and you're willing to take ownership for all the unique events, situations, and circumstances that uniquely bother you.

If you think that everyone is experiencing the same bothers as you are, you might be tempted to be passive and wait for someone else to come along and figure out how to handle them. But since you know that only you are experiencing your specific bothers, you know that you need to take unique, individual action to transform them.

You claim 100 percent responsibility for your unique bothers, and that immediately gives you control over what you're going to do about them.

We're all the same.

To be human is to be bothered. The reason for this is simple to understand when you recognize that there are eight billion people on the planet. Each of us is busily trying to make our lives better in ways that end up causing changes in other people's lives. Their changes can bother you, and your changes can bother them.

Anytime you change your behavior, it's going to impact other people's lives. You want to do it in a way that doesn't impede teamwork and cooperation, but at the same time, you're not responsible for how other people react to your changes. That's their bother, not yours.

You can be conscious of the ways in which you're impacting others, but you don't have to take responsibility for how they react. Our lives are not static; we're always trying to make them better. We're always expanding our influence.

Changes that we're the cause of don't tend to bother us. It's having to come to grips with other changes that is the source of our bother. And sometimes, it's when we're not making the changes we want to make that we feel bothered.

We're all uniquely different.

Other people are bothered, and you're bothered—but not in the same way. You have a whole lifetime of unique experiences you're always working to make sense of. No one else knows what "making sense" means to you. As a result, what bothers you is uniquely yours and different from what bothers everyone else.

We're in a lifetime process of continually making sense of things in the moment. We make sense of our experience, and based on that, we make decisions, we communicate, we take action, we achieve results, and we have a sense of progress and achievement. And out of that, we develop bigger ambitions.

We're in a constant process of growing, but allowing ourselves to be bothered impedes our growth. It's vital to transform our bothers and create breakthroughs in order to keep progressing. To the degree that we don't transform, we say stay stuck.

Yours to deal with.

You're essentially alone with all of your own bothers. That's a fact whether you like it or not, so you might as well like it! But, not only like it—actually love it. Love the fact that you get to deal with all of your bothers as your own unique property because you can create amazing breakthroughs.

You can't anticipate when you're going to be surprised, but you can choose to not dread change and the inevitable bother that comes with it. You can look forward to the transformation.

What holds some entrepreneurs back is that using your bothers for transformation and growth isn't necessarily difficult. Humans are good at making a virtue of necessity, and for most of human history, work was hard.

If you're one of the many entrepreneurs who thinks that work can only be meaningful if it's hard, you have to change that thinking. Otherwise, your biggest obstacle as an entrepreneur might be that you won't allow "easy" to have any meaning.

Taking complete ownership.

You now have an extraordinary possibility. Up until now, you've seen your bothers as something negative. Now, there's a sudden possibility that every one of them can be valuable raw material for creating positive progress.

There's no use in trying to fight the fact that you own your bothers. There's no benefit in blaming someone else for your bothers and wanting that other person to take responsibility for stopping them. The more you take ownership, the more your progress accelerates.

By taking ownership, you've freed everyone else from responsibility for what bothers you. This actually simplifies the task enormously. If other people have to be involved, it gets more complicated. When you take 100 percent responsibility for your bothers, you can move forward and transform them using your best knowledge, best experience, and best skills.

If you hold someone else responsible, you won't fully use your own transformative capabilities.

Unique bothers, unique breakthroughs.

This is a huge switch of mindset. You've always looked at your bothers one way, and now you can look at them totally differently. Instead of complaining about your bothers and trying to get rid of them, now you'll welcome them. Every one of them can now be a breakthrough.

You won't be able to predict every situation that comes along, but you'll be prepared for unexpected situations, and you'll know how best to deal with them.

When new circumstances arise, and other people seem stuck because of them, you'll know right away what you should do, which is take action to make unexpected progress in the unexpected situation.

BOTHER BOTHER BOTHER BOTHER
BOTHER BOTHER BOTHER BOTHER
BOTHER BOTHER BOTHER BOTHER
ALL HUMANS
HAVE BOTHERS

SITUATIONS
EVENTS
WORRIES
WAITING
WEATHER
YOUR BOTHERS ARE UNIQUELY YOURS

Chapter 4

If You Weren't Bothered

You have a sudden breakthrough: Every time you're bothered, you ask yourself, "If this didn't bother me, what would I be doing?"

You've successfully developed many positive habits in your life, each enabling you to achieve progress and growth. Well, here's another great habit you can add to your repertoire. Every time you feel bothered—by anything—automatically ask yourself the following question:

"If this didn't bother me, what would I be doing?"

Instantly, something remarkable occurs. Your mind switches to an image of a productive task you can achieve right now and puts your brain back into full power. As you go into action, you no longer feel bothered.

Bothers paralyze you.

What you hate most about being bothered is the experience of being paralyzed. Emotion overwhelms your natural ability to think, decide, plan, and take action. You feel stuck. And in the past—actually, right up until now—being bothered caused you to suddenly feel helpless. But not anymore.

Feeling paralyzed isn't fun. You can't think straight, you can't plan, you can't make a decision, and you can't take action. This is one of the worst feelings for human beings. But there's nothing going on outside of you that can explain why you're reacting this way. It's strictly internal.

And now you know that when you get stuck, you can respond to the situation by asking yourself this question. And just like that, your brain is no longer stuck. What's more, you've given your brain direction. You've zeroed in on something that needs to be done, and it's given you a tremendous amount of energy to act very quickly and get it done.

You might be thinking, "Yes, but there are real problems behind the bother." And that's true. But you encounter problems all the time that don't cause you to feel stuck and bothered. When you react emotionally to a problem, that's when it becomes a bother, and the only way out is to figure out what you would do, what action you would take to move forward, if you weren't bothered.

You were lacking this skill, and now you have this go-to solution anytime you find yourself bothered by a situation. Whatever the bother was about, what was *really* bothering you was that you felt paralyzed. After you've asked yourself the question and gotten unstuck, when you revisit the bother, you'll find you no longer feel paralyzed.

A single question frees you up.

You now have an immediate way out. As soon as you feel bothered, you'll have trained yourself to automatically ask yourself, "If this didn't bother me, what would I be doing?" In a matter of seconds, your mind is released from the trap and focuses your attention on fast action to achieve a positive result.

Going into motion is the answer. It's the solution to paralysis. It gives you a feeling of relief when you do it, and it lets your brain do what it does well, which is to focus and create measurable progress. When you're bothered, it's like you're in a prison. But when you flip the switch by asking yourself the question, you suddenly have access to all of your experiences and capabilities. Instead of being trapped by an emotional reaction, you're responding in a practical way in order to achieve a breakthrough.

Your nervous system was triggered by the bother, and you went into fight-or-flight mode, but when you ask yourself what you would do if you weren't bothered, it causes you to think cognitively rather than emotionally about how to respond in a useful way, getting you out of that triggered state.

From stuck to breakthrough.

You're amazed at how quickly you master this, even more so because you're now equipped to successfully transform every bother for the rest of your life. Simply put, every bother you encounter from now on will be an opportunity to create great new breakthroughs.

You weren't born thinking like this, but the human brain is incredible, allowing you to adopt the mindset in almost no time at all. And like riding a bike, you're not going to forget how to do it. In fact, you're only going to get better and better at transforming your bothers into breakthrough actions.

So not only do you feel no need to complain about your bothers, you get breakthroughs as payoffs for identifying and transforming them.

Rethinking past bothers.

Suddenly, your sense of your future is intriguing and exciting. And an equally positive new perspective can now be applied to your past. Everything that bothered you back then, right up until yesterday, was also something that could have been transformed into a breakthrough.

With every single occasion in the past when you were bothered and got out of it but didn't get clear on why you were bothered, you can revisit that situation and ask, "If I hadn't been bothered then, what would I have done?"

This recontextualizes something that you previously thought was negative, and it emphasizes the power of the question-asking, bother-transforming skill you have now but didn't have then. With mastery of this skill, you can stop complaining in the present and remove all blame for the past.

Everything's just opportunity.

Your experience in all situations is entirely your own unique property that you can use for your own purposes. Some of your experience will always bother you. Until now, this really bothered you! But no more. You now respond to every bother with an instantly transformative question.

You used to think of bothers as negatives. Now, you not only know how to turn a negative into a positive, you recognize that the negative itself can have great value. If the bother hadn't been there, you wouldn't have been able to create something positive from it.

You know that as long as you're growing, you're going to experience bothers. This doesn't trouble you, because you know that every bother is an opportunity to create something new and valuable.

THIS DOESN'T WORK...
BOTHER BOTHER BOT

...THIS ALWAYS DOES
IF I WEREN'T BOTHERED...

Chapter 5

90% Of Any Solution

You suddenly realize that all problems in your life are always 90% made up of bothers you haven't yet transformed.

At this point, you might be thinking, "Life can't be this simple!" Well, that all depends. It depends on how you've been dealing with all of your bothers before reading this book. If you're already using the "If this didn't bother me" question, and it works every time you use it, doesn't that simplify the way you look at your future?

And if you'd mastered this capability in the past, wouldn't that have simplified how you remember your past problems and bothers? Ninety percent of your lifetime problems were caused by not transforming your bothers.

Many people go through their lives without ever coming to this realization. Their bothers just keep stacking up, making it more and more difficult for them to navigate effectively in the present.

You also create your problems.

When you're clear and confident, problems are challenges that energize you.

But the problems that drain your energy, that frustrate you most, come from the build-up of many bothers you've failed to transform. These problems are created because you haven't been in the habit of transforming your bothers.

You can now fix the problem of having untransformed bothers by revisiting them and asking yourself the question, "If I hadn't been bothered in this situation, what would I have done instead?" You trust in the question, and you trust your answers. And by doing this, you turn one negative after another into a positive, and you free yourself from the burden of past bothers.

This is how you heal yourself from having carried around all of those past negative experiences in the present. And now, all the bothers you experience are going to be transformed into solutions, which means that you'll never again have problems as a result of untransformed bothers.

Past, present, and future.

You may have spent a lot of your life so far complaining about your problems to anyone who would listen to you. But now that you realize that most of your so-called problems are actually your creation, your entire understanding of your life—looking back, right now, and looking forward—is entirely yours.

And it's unlimited. The amount of your experience is such that you're never going to run out of it while you're alive. You know that bothers are never going to stop appearing, which is fine because you're not looking to avoid bothers. You accept that there will always be bothers, and whenever there are, you take the experience of being bothered and make it serve your purposes.

No more complaining.

Since you now realize it will no longer be necessary to complain about any of your problems, you can see that listening to other people's problems is a waste of time. You're not going to listen to their problems because you know what the issue is. They're bothered.

Anything they tell you about their problem is made up by them to try to explain why they're not coming to grips with their own sense of bother. The main desire of a lot of people nowadays, including on social media, is to unload their problems onto other people and wait for those people to rescue them. But you understand how bother actually works, and you're not in the business of performing rescues. You don't ask for them, and you don't offer them.

When you rescue someone, you've given them permission not to be skillful. And you weaken their ability to take responsibility for themselves. You've told them that the first thing they should look for when they're in trouble is for someone to rescue them.

Now that you've mastered the "bother question" for yourself, you can use it every time someone else complains. Simply ask them, "If this didn't bother you, what would you be doing?"

The question snaps them out of the bothered state so they can step back and evaluate the situation objectively. With that clarity, they can see the next step they need to take to move forward.

10% is great!

You've now figured out what causes 90 percent of any problem, but what about the ten percent of a problem that still exists? The ten percent is a wonderfully positive challenge for you to grow your teamwork capabilities. Each individual takes care of their own 90 percent, and together, everyone solves the other ten percent.

You're not asking anyone to *solve* the problems that bother you. What you're asking is for everybody to *cooperate* in this process of transforming your bothers by using their capabilities to leverage yours. The other 10 percent of the problem is taken care of through teamwork and communication.

If it works for you, you know that it can work for anyone, so this formula will allow each individual to handle 90 percent of any problem that comes up. And everyone working together with the mindset of wanting to solve problems means that the other ten percent will always get taken care of as well.

Time to break free.

If other people around you are learning how to transform their own bothers and are increasingly solving their own problems, that will be an extra bonus. But whether they do or don't, you can quickly move forward on your own. Every day from now on, you'll be transforming all your bothers. You're already breaking free.

You're granting yourself freedom, and you're extending that freedom to every other individual. What everyone else does with that freedom is their choice, and your freedom is never dependent on someone else doing the same thing.

You can test your beliefs by asking, "Am I happy with this belief even if no one else in the world believes it?" With the answer of "yes," you know that you can carry on with this belief independently. You don't have to spend any time or energy trying to convince anyone that your belief is valid. All that matters is that your belief is useful.

BREAKING FREE
IF THIS DIDN'T BOTHER ME...
90% OF THE PROBLEM

BREAKING THROUGH
BREAK-THROUGH
SOLUTION!
90% OF THE SOLUTION
REALLY, REALLY, REALLY SMART!

Chapter 6

Bothered People Congregate

You're clear that what bothers you is uniquely yours, and you're committed to keeping all of your bothers to yourself.

You've noticed that many people organize themselves around their bothers. They want to tell everyone else what's bothering them, and they let others tell them about even more kinds of bother. But now that you realize what causes your own bothers, you know it's very important to keep these to yourself.

You're amazed that everything that bothers you is actually valuable raw material for your own growth and for creating your own breakthroughs. You realize that the people you know who are always organizing their lives around their bothers and listening to everybody else's bothers are totally on the wrong path.

The people who are getting together to share their bothers think they have something in common with one another. What they don't realize is that each individual's bothers are unique, as they relate to each person's unique life experiences. These individuals haven't taken responsibility for their bothers. Instead, they blame outside factors.

They like gathering because they like complaining and sharing the blame. They don't want to feel alone and as though they're the only one bothered by what's bothering them.

Your bothers are yours.

You're now finding it humorous remembering how you used to congregate with other people in order to share one another's bothers. It's not just the waste of time that amazes you now but that all the bothers in your life were your own unique opportunities to grow—and you didn't take advantage of them.

When you experience a bother, it's likely because it reminds you of something you experienced in the past. No one else has access to your experiences, so no one can experience a bother as you do, and no one else can be responsible for your bother. You can't blame anyone else.

You won't be missing anything by no longer getting together with other people to talk about your bothers. And you won't be alone. Instead of congregating with bothered people, you'll band together with like-minded individuals who have taken full responsibility for their own bothers as you have.

Avoiding bothered crowds.

You're now totally clear that from this moment forward, you're never again going to relate to other people on the basis of bothers—neither yours nor theirs. That's because you know "bothered crowds" are a total waste of time for everyone involved. You're going to transform your bothers yourself.

Problems are real, but the way each person experiences bother because of a problem is unique. A group of people telling each other what's bothering them isn't going to accomplish anything.

If you're going to be useful in solving problems, you have to take responsibility for what bothers you. And you can help bothered people by demonstrating to them that they can take responsibility for, and transform, their own bothers.

Boring and meaningless.

You suddenly realize that what you thought was important and fascinating about people congregating around their bothers is actually boring and meaningless for you. Every time you pay attention to other people's bothers, you're missing the opportunity to transform something that bothers you and experience a breakthrough.

There will always be people who prefer to complain than to do anything about what's bothering them. This is a case of adults engaging in adolescent behavior. It happens, but it's inappropriate for these people's ages, and there's nothing useful that can come out of their insistence on being this way.

Only they are responsible for their lack of progress. You don't have to accept it. You don't have to be part of their groups. In fact, you know that transforming bothers takes individual initiative.

There's a sense of oppression and alienation that always accompanies chronically bothered people. But when you take responsibility for your own bothers and make progress by transforming them, you no longer feel oppressed or alienated.

No more fear of being alone.

You're aware that the entire reason you've been attracted to being around bothered people was because you were afraid of being alone with your own bothers. But now you're totally clear that only by being alone can you transform anything that bothers you.

Being with other people's bothers is something you used to desire because it was a distraction, and it felt easier than being alone with your bothers. It took your mind off your bothers, which have always seemed worse when no one else was around.

But being with other people's bothers introduces complexity, complication, and confusion, with no clarity and no solution. It obfuscates the real issues, which are your bothers and your bothers alone. Your bothers are no longer something you want to escape from, but something you recognize you have to transform—and transform by yourself.

Instantly independent.

Now that you're willing to be alone with your own unique bothers, you realize that you're instantly independent of everyone else's bothers. You've never seen this before, but now your whole "life of bother" becomes permanently understandable. You can now take complete ownership of every bother in your life.

You recognize that this ownership is a good thing. It means that all of the meaning behind all of your experiences of bother is what you give it. You're not waiting around, hoping that someone else will come along, transform your bothers for you, and give your experiences meaning.

You're making the decision that you'll give meaning to all your experiences. The meaning of your experiences will never be determined by an outside factor. And you recognize that not only you but every individual has the power to take this responsibility for turning their bothers into breakthroughs.

IT'S CONTAGIOUS
BOTHER BOTHER BOTHER
BOTHER BOTHER BOTHER
YEAH, THAT'S MY BOTHER!
MINE, TOO!
OH YEAH, LET ME IN THERE!

IT'S USEFUL
YOUR BOTHER
AHH...

Chapter 7

Transforming Your Bothers

You're committed to transforming every bother into positive growth, and you immediately meet others who are doing the same.

In the past, you've shared your bothers with other people and received a full dose in return, which made your bothers even worse. But that was in the past, before you recognized that your bothers are uniquely yours. Now, you're thinking about all the bothers in your life from a positive perspective.

Instead of seeing them as a burden that you unload onto others, you see your bothers as opportunities. The moment you decide to transform all your bothers in this way, you immediately begin to attract other transformers.

Like attracts like. This is true in physics as well as in humanity. Humans are social creatures, and we're attracted to things that resemble us. If you're bothered, you're looking for other bothered people because that's common ground. Now that you know to transform your bothers in a positive way, you'll be looking for other people with like mindsets.

You've stopped doing that.

You feel a bit surprised and uncomfortable when you realize how often in the past you wasted time and effort complaining about your bothers with other bothered people.

But now you're equally relieved and happy that you no longer do that. You're freeing yourself from all those old relationships. It didn't get you anywhere, and now you're past doing it. Instead of wasting time complaining in groups, you've taken responsibility for your bothers.

Other people are going to continue complaining about their bothers and getting nowhere, but doing that just doesn't hold any interest for you anymore.

Once you get past the initial fear, uncertainty, and discomfort that can come with making a change, you won't miss spending time with complainers. You don't want to take them along on your new, transformative path.

Endlessly negative networks.

As you take greater responsibility for your bothers, you become keenly aware of the way that so many other people are trapped in negative networks of endless complaining about their bothers, and this is multiplied by technology. You're now celebrating what bothers you as building blocks for growth.

Unless you create your own conscious network, chances are that you'll end up in negative networks. In other words, you'll be around people whose default position is to see their bothers as being caused from the outside. And that's ripe opportunity for blaming and complaining. So, as you go along, you're creating a separation.

One thing that holds people back is fear of being alone with their bothers. They feel defenseless when they think their bothers are coming from an outside source, and they need the protection of others' company. They want to commiserate with other bothered people. But once you know that all your bothers come from the inside, you can take responsibility for them and determine what they mean. As soon as you do this, you're operating in a whole new world.

Like-minded transformers.

From the very moment you decide to take control of your own bothers, it seems that you immediately begin encountering like-minded people who are also using their unique bothers to transform themselves.

It's like you've switched to a new frequency on the radio, and you're now picking up on what other people who share your new approach are doing. This is a huge breakthrough. You're inspired by them, and they're motivated by what you're achieving.

You don't even have to know what these other people are transforming. It's enough for you to recognize that they're fellow transformers. You'll experience commonality with one another. It's a much better society to be a part of.

You feel this is a reward for leaving behind the complainers you used to spend time with. You may be alone in your responsibility for transforming your own bothers, but you've joined networks of people doing the same thing. Instead of being based on negativity, these networks are based on excitement. And they're endless.

Also, because of technology, it's easier now than ever to connect with like-minded people.

Accelerating daily progress.

It's totally clear to you why it was almost impossible for you to make personal progress when you were surrounded by other bothered people who were blaming and complaining.

Now that you're being reinforced by positive transformers,

you feel yourself using your bothers to quickly transform yourself. With every bother, instead of becoming confused, you create value. Instead of being reactive, you're creative. Instead of staying in a negative space, you turn it into something positive.

You're either on this path or you're on the other path. It's binary. You wouldn't be doing yourself any favors if you were only halfway on the path of making accelerated daily progress. You have no motivation to be anything less than 100 percent committed to this approach because you know that the other path won't take you where you want to go.

Courage creates capability.

As you discover the reason why your life is improving in so many positive ways, you also appreciate the courage you've demonstrated in coming to creative grips with all your bothers. Many bothered people never do this. And your endless reward for being brave is an entirely creative, more capable future.

No one forced you to do this. It was entirely out of choice. And it took a fair amount of courage for you to completely cut off the possibility of blaming any outside factors for the bothers you experience.

You didn't have to do this, and many people don't do this, but now that you've been courageous and done it, you'll experience constant, ever-increasing rewards for it.

EVERY BOTHER IS...
BREAK-
THROUGH
BOTHER
YOU TRANSFORMING

...A BREAKTHROUGH
PROGRESS
TEAMWORK
CREATIVITY
ACHIEVEMENT
FOCUS
OTHERS TRANSFORMING

Chapter 8

Loving Your Bothers

You permanently realize that everything that bothers you is a unique opportunity to create an ingenious breakthrough.

You hated your bothers, and now each one of them is a new best friend. The more you enjoy and creatively engage with your bothers, the more you appreciate yourself. What makes you uniquely interesting and useful to others lies in owning all your bothers as uniquely yours.

Indeed, the more you take ownership of what bothers you, the more you become uniquely creative and confident in every area of your life. It may seem like a fanciful trick, but it turns out to be one of the most crucial skills of your life.

Second-guessing yourself takes up a lot of energy. On the other hand, when you engage with a bother by asking yourself, "What would I be doing if I weren't bothered?" you get an enormous amount of energy from the activity within moments.

What a switch!

An hour ago, maybe less, you thought that bothers were always, well, bothersome! They were just one negative thing after another for as long as you can remember. Then, suddenly, with a single change of mindset, everything's completely different. Every bother is a great opportunity.

We have an amazing ability to use insight gained in a single moment. We can use it to reevaluate and change the meaning of vast stretches of our lives. All in a split second.

You don't have to do this, and you can't force anyone else

to do this. But if you do make this incredibly quick mindset shift, you'll see an enormous jump in opportunities and positive outcomes. All you have to do is make the switch by taking personal responsibility for all your bothers. And your skill at transforming your bothers will continually increase as you do it.

Bothered is just the start.

If you're willing to look back, you'll see that all of your best and most creative breakthroughs likely started out as bothers. You just don't remember actually transforming each negative situation into a new, positive jump by breaking out of your bothered state and focusing on taking action.

You might have a fear that if you pay attention to your bothers, you won't have time to pay attention to anything else. The fact is, though, you're already paying attention to a lot of things that aren't necessarily useful for you. There are likely bothers you experienced years ago that still bother you when you think of them. Certainly, that's a waste of time. After all, you're the only one who knows about it. No one else has the foggiest idea.

But here you are, years later, wasting time being bothered by something you didn't transform. But if you imagine a situation from the past and consider what you could have done differently if you hadn't been bothered, the moment your mind is satisfied with the answer, you're clear and free. You can let the bother go.

Over time and with practice, you'll develop an intelligence about which things are worth transforming and which things you can just let go of.

Just answering the question, "If this didn't bother me, what would I be doing?" immediately puts you into motion, and that action gets rid of the bother. You've transformed it.

Four-stage ingenuity.

Here's how it always goes:

1. Something bothers you.
2. You ask yourself the question, "If this didn't bother me, what would I be doing?"
3. You visualize a new course of action.
4. You complete the action.

As the saying goes: Apply, lather, rinse, repeat. A few seconds of bother can turn into hours of creativity.

This takes practice. It's like you've fallen off a bike again and again, and now that you've had enough of doing that, you're going to master what it takes to stay on the bike. Your bothers may have stopped you in your tracks in the past, but now you'll master transforming those bothers into action.

Most won't do this.

If you're suddenly worried that you're only now discovering something that everyone else already knew, don't be. That thought is just a bother. And as the formula goes above, "If you weren't bothered, what would you be doing?" You'll immediately be on to your next creative breakthrough. And the truth is, hardly anyone else knows this, anyway.

The fact that most people don't use this process has nothing to do with what you're doing. You have the mindset and the formula to transform your bothers in any situation.

People who are stuck in the same old trap because they haven't taken responsibility for transforming their own bothers are not your responsibility. But when you come across someone else who is a fellow bother transformer, you'll both be drawn to the idea of collaborating together.

Unlimited opportunity ahead.

What all of this really means is that with the simple mindset change outlined in this very short book, your life ahead will become dramatically more productive and meaningful than how you remember your past. Where your life before might have been a hard slog, everything ahead is exciting opportunity.

There's a freedom in this that's very different from the way most people think about freedom. Freedom doesn't mean setting up your life so that you're never bothered. That's just buying into the idea that bothers come from the outside.

Since you're aware that your bothers come from inside of you and that you have the power to either transform your bothers into opportunity or get stuck by your bothers, you'll never be in the position that so many others are: prevented from moving forward and complaining about it.

You have to acknowledge that you're the creator of your own bother. And when you have an immediate solution to being bothered, that gives you a great deal of freedom.

ENDLESS BOTHERS
1 SOMETHING BOTHERS YOU
SNAP!
2 YOU ASK...
IF THIS DIDN'T BOTHER ME...
WHAT WOULD I BE DOING?

ENDLESS INGENUITY
4 YOU COMPLETE THE ACTION
!!!
3 YOU VISUALIZE A NEW COURSE OF ACTION
!!!
A
B

Conclusion

Freedom In A Bothered World

You've freed yourself up for a remarkable future that most people cannot achieve, pulling off an extraordinary thinking trick.

Most people strive for greater freedom, which they think comes from being protected from outside bother. The mistake here is that everyone's bother comes from the inside.

You totally grasp and appreciate this—so much so that you're now increasingly enthusiastic about your bothers. It's your full engagement with your unique bothers that enables you to continually increase your personal freedom in all areas of your life.

No one could do this for you. It's something you've had to do yourself. And while you can't force anyone else to make the change that you have, and you're not responsible for whether anyone else takes responsibility for transforming their own bothers, others will be able to follow your example.

If they don't, you can't let yourself become frustrated by that because that would mean your solution is now generating a bother for you.

Enormous time savings.

In the past, you've experienced all of your bothers as wasted time that makes you feel guilty when you think about it. Not just minutes and hours were wasted, but whole days and weeks. Now, with your new approach, no bother can last more than a few seconds before you transform it into an energizing breakthrough.

You're not going to be held back anymore, paralyzed from making decisions and taking action. Bothers will always be there, but they'll never again make you feel stuck, because you now recognize that every bother represents an opportunity.

From now on, you'll respond to every bother you experience by going into productive action and turning the bother you're experiencing into progress.

Multiplying your money.

You'll increasingly be creating breakthroughs out of your own bothers and helping others to do the same. That's where all the best opportunities are in the 21st century—instead of in selling products and services, it's going to be in providing solutions to new bothers that are created by new ventures.

If you're the person who's always creating unique personal breakthroughs, you'll automatically become an incredibly useful person to others. We all make our living by finding solutions, and, basically, all business involves helping other people solve problems they're too bothered by to even understand.

When you develop the ability to transform your bothers, it communicates to the outside world that you're someone who can objectively look at a situation without allowing negative emotions to prevent you from strategizing and innovating. And the better you become at breaking out of bothered states and taking action, the more you're able to create new solutions that are useful for other people.

Collaborating with other transformers.

As you transform your own bothers, you attract the collaboration of others who are transforming theirs. All of you are creating uniquely unpredictable breakthroughs that are easy to combine. The expanding collaboration is energizing because everyone takes responsibility for their own bothers.

You know that in this situation, your collaborators are never going to point blame at you and are never going to expect you to solve their bothers. These are safe collaborations, which means you're free to focus on using your best capabilities and creativity.

When people who are at their best work together, it's a real pleasure. As you become adept at transforming your bothers, and increasingly engage in collaborations with like-minded others who transform their own bothers, you'll come to dislike collaborating with individuals who waste time by complaining about their bothers and who blame others for their feelings of bother.

Powerful accelerating purpose.

The more that each individual involved in a collaboration masters their transformation, the more that everyone experiences an energizing common purpose. Your morale keeps rising, your momentum keeps increasing, and your motivation keeps growing. Your individual uniqueness keeps reinforcing everyone else's.

Each person is making unique breakthroughs that serve the project and every person collaborating on it. By definition, no unique capabilities and no unique breakthroughs are alike.

This means that not only is there no blame between collaborators, there's no competition either.

You use your uniqueness, and everyone else uses theirs. You never have to wonder or worry about what your collaborators are doing because you trust that they're going to get their jobs done in their own way and transform any bothers that might cause them to get stuck.

Each individual is using their best capabilities, and all the capabilities are connecting to uniquely reach the collaborators' common goal. You'll always be fascinated to see what your collaborators have transformed because there are only solutions, no complaining, in what they're doing.

Everything frees you up.

You realize that everything you needed to create a life of freedom has been available to you from the very beginning. Your unique freedom lies in your unique bothers. As soon as you own your bothers, you become freer and happier. It's hard to believe at first, but now you're totally certain.

For people who don't have this skill, every bother becomes a new drama. But once you get used to transforming your bothers, you see that there's a sameness about all bothers that allows you to instantly recognize and transform them.

You'll always have bothers in your life, but the big shift here is the amount of time that you stay stuck. You're now able to recognize your bothers for what they are—emotional reactions to situations—and break out of them more quickly, freeing you up to take action.

GREAT PURPOSE
BREAK-
THROUGHS
FREEDOM
FREEDOM
BREAK-
THROUGHS
BREAK-
THROUGHS

GREAT COLLABORATION
FREEDOM
BREAK-THROUGHS
BREAK-THROUGHS
FREEDOM
BREAK-THROUGHS

The Strategic Coach Program

For Ambitious, Collaborative Entrepreneurs

You commit to growing upward through three transformative levels, giving yourself 25 years to exponentially improve every aspect of your work and life.

Not Being Bothered is a crucial capability and a natural result of everything we coach in The Strategic Coach Program, a workshop experience for successful entrepreneurs who are committed and devoted to business and industry transformation for the long-term, for 25 years and beyond.

The Program has a destination for all participants—creating more and more of what we call "Free Zone Frontiers." This means taking advantage of your own unique capabilities, the unique capabilities around you, your unique opportunities, and your unique circumstances, and putting the emphasis on creating a life that is free of competition.

Most entrepreneurs grow up in a system where they think competition is the name of the game. The general way of looking at the world is that the natural state of affairs is competition, and collaboration is an anomaly.

Free Zone Frontier

The Free Zone Frontier is a whole new level of entrepreneurship that many people don't even know is possible. But once you start putting the framework in place, new possibilities open up for you. You create zones that are purely about collaboration. You start recognizing that collaboration is the natural state, and competition is the anomaly. It makes you look at things totally differently.

Strategic Coach has continually created concepts and thinking tools that allow entrepreneurs to more and more see their future in terms of Free Zones that have no competition.

Three levels of entrepreneurial growth.

Strategic Coach participants continually transform how they think, make decisions, communicate, and take action based on their use of dozens of unique entrepreneurial mindsets we've developed. The Program has been refined through decades of entrepreneurial testing and is the most concentrated, massive discovery process in the world created solely for transformative entrepreneurs who want to create new Free Zones.

Over the years, we've observed that our clients' development happens in levels of mastery. And so, we've organized the Program into three levels of participation, each of which involves two different types of transformation:

The Signature Level. The first level is devoted to your *personal* transformation, which has to do with how you're spending your time as an entrepreneur as well as how you're taking advantage of your personal freedom outside of business that your entrepreneurial success affords you. Focusing on improving yourself on a personal level before you move on to making significant changes in other aspects of your life and business is key because you have to simplify before you can multiply.

The second aspect of the Signature Level is how you look at your *teamwork*. This means seeing that your future consists of teamwork with others whose unique capabilities complement your own, leading to bigger and better goals that constantly get achieved at a measurably higher rate.

The 10x Ambition Level. Once you feel confident about your own personal transformation and have access to ever-expanding teamwork, you can think much bigger in terms of your *company*. An idea that at one time would have seemed scary and even impossible—growing your business 10x—is no longer a wild dream but a result of the systematic expansion of the teamwork model you've established. And because you're stable in the center, you won't get thrown off balance by exponential growth. Your life stays balanced and integrated even as things grow around you.

And that's when you're in a position to transform your relationship with your *market*. This is when your company has a huge impact on the marketplace that competitors can't even understand because they're not going through this transformative structure or thinking in terms of 25 years as you are. Thinking in terms of 25 years gives you an expansive sense of freedom and the ability to have big picture goals.

The Free Zone Frontier Level. Once you've mastered the first four areas of transformation, you're at the point where your company is self-managing and self-multiplying, which means that your time can now be totally freed up. At this stage, competitors become collaborators and it becomes all about your *industry*. You can consider everything you've created as a single capability you can now match up with another company's to create collaborations that go way beyond 10x.

And, finally, it becomes *global*. You immediately see that there are possibilities of going global—it's just a matter of combining your capabilities with those of others to create something exponentially bigger than you could ever have achieved on your own.

Global collaborative community.

Entrepreneurism can be a lonely activity. You have goals that the people you grew up with don't understand. Your family might not comprehend you at all and don't know why you keep wanting to expand, why you want to take new risks, why you want to jump to the next level. And so it becomes proportionately more important as you gain your own individual mastery that you're in a community of thousands of individuals who are on exactly the same journey.

In The Strategic Coach Program, you benefit from not only your own continual individual mastery but from the constant expansion of support from and collaboration with a growing global community of extraordinarily liberated entrepreneurs who will increasingly share with you their deep wisdom and creative breakthroughs as innovators in hundreds of different industries and markets.

If you've reached a jumping off point in your entrepreneurial career where you're beyond ready to multiply all of your capabilities and opportunities into a 10x more creative and productive formula that keeps getting simpler and more satisfying, we're ready for you.

For more information and to register for The Strategic Coach Program, call 416.531.7399 or 1.800.387.3206, or visit us online at *strategiccoach.com*.

THREE LEVELS OF

FREE ZONE FRONTIER

- 100x Collaboration
- Perfect Fit VISION
- 25-Year Hero Target
- 100% Simplifier/Multiplier
- $15-Trillion Free Zone

10X AMBITION

- Self-Multiplying Company
- Simplifier/Multiplier
- Total Cash Confidence
- Always Be The Buyer
- The D.O.S. Conversation

SIGNATURE

- Self-Managing Company
- The Lifetime Extender
- Free, Focus, and Buffer Days
- Unique Ability Teamwork
- The Largest Cheque

FREE ZONE

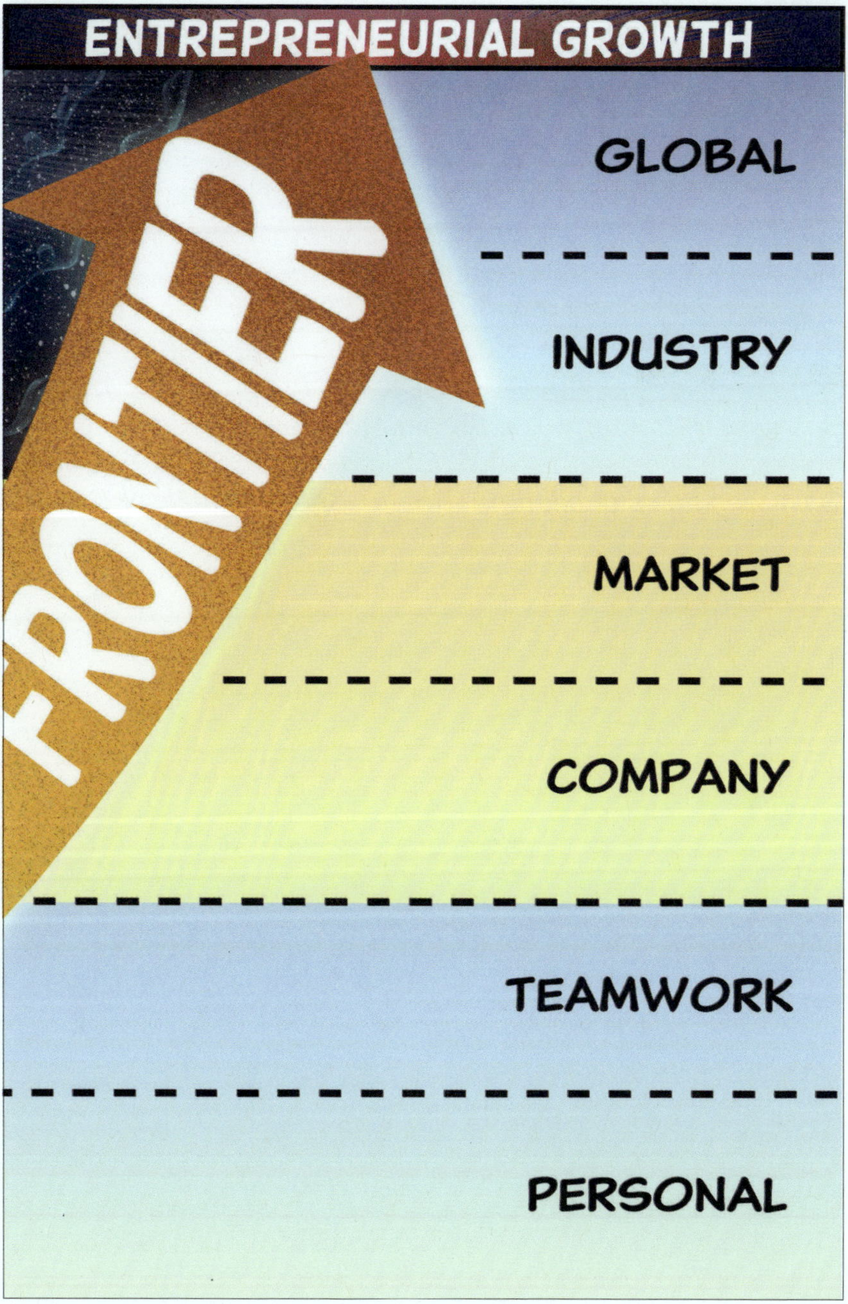

ENTREPRENEURIAL GROWTH

FRONTIER

GLOBAL

INDUSTRY

MARKET

COMPANY

TEAMWORK

PERSONAL

About The Author

Dan Sullivan

Dan Sullivan is the founder and president of The Strategic Coach Inc. and creator of The Strategic Coach® Program, which helps accomplished entrepreneurs reach new heights of success and happiness. He is author of over 50 publications, including *The Great Crossover, The 21st Century Agent, Creative Destruction, How The Best Get Better*, and The Ambition Series of quarterly small books. He is co-author of *Who Not How, The Gap And The Gain, The Laws of Lifetime Growth*, and *The Advisor Century*.